Rachel Carson
PIONEER OF ECOLOGY

P9-CCR-796

"Man is a part of nature, and his war against nature is
. . . a war against himself."   —Rachel Carson

Rachel Carson

PIONEER OF ECOLOGY

By Kathleen V. Kudlinski

Illustrated by Ted Lewin

PUFFIN BOOKS

For Hank
husband, friend

PUFFIN BOOKS

A Division of Penguin Books USA Inc.
375 Hudson Street, New York, New York 10014
Penguin Books Ltd, 27 Wrights Lane, London W8 5TZ, England
Penguin Books Australia Ltd, Ringwood, Victoria, Australia
Penguin Books Canada Ltd, 10 Alcorn Avenue, Toronto, Ontario, Canada M4V 3B2
Penguin Books (N.Z.) Ltd, 182–190 Wairau Road, Auckland 10, New Zealand

Penguin Books Ltd, Registered Offices: Harmondsworth, Middlesex, England

First published in the United States of America by Viking Penguin,
a division of Penguin Books USA Inc., 1988
Published in Puffin Books 1989
14   16   18   20   19   17   15   13
Text copyright © Kathleen V. Kudlinski, 1988
Illustrations copyright © Ted Lewin, 1988
All rights reserved
Women of Our Time® is a registered trademark of Viking Penguin,
a division of Penguin Books USA Inc.

Grateful acknowledgment is made for permission to reprint excerpts from Rachel Carson's
"Who I Am and Why I Came to P.C.W.," her letters to Mary Frye,
and Dr. William Beebee. Reproduced by permission of
Frances Collin, Trustee. Copyright © Roger Christie, 1988.
Further acknowledgment is made to the Collection of American Literature,
The Beinecke Rare Book and Manuscript Library, Yale University
for access to use the Rachel Carson papers owned by them.

LIBRARY OF CONGRESS CATALOGING-IN-PUBLICATION DATA
Kudlinski, Kathleen V.   Rachel Carson : pioneer of ecology / by Kathleen V. Kudlinski :
illustrated by Ted Lewin.   p.   cm.   ISBN 0-14-032242-6
1. Carson, Rachel, 1907–1964—Juvenile literature.   2. Ecologists—
United States—Biography—Juvenile literature.   I. Lewin, Ted.   II. Title.
[QH31.C33K83   1989]   574'.092'4—dc19   [B]   89-30216

Printed in the United States of America
Set in Garamond #3

CONTENTS

Rachel Carson

PIONEER OF ECOLOGY

1

Dreams of the Sea

Rachel pressed the conch shell to her ear, and dreamed of the distant, vast sea. At age seven, she knew that the magical hiss and murmuring sounds inside the shell were just echoes of the pulse in her own ear. Still, she liked to pretend it was waves rushing on a beach.

For most people living far from the ocean, a conch was just a lovely trinket, but it meant much more to Rachel. "As a very small child I was fascinated by the ocean, though I had never seen it," she said later. "I dreamed of it and longed to see it . . ."

She would never have dreamed that, through her books, she would share the magic of the seas with millions of people around the world. All she knew, as she watched her mother put the shell back over the fireplace, was that someday, somehow, she would see the ocean.

Rachel spent a lot of time with her mother. Mrs. Carson often kept her home from the elementary school in Springdale, Pennsylvania. Sometimes it was because a classmate was ill and Mrs. Carson was afraid Rachel would catch one of the deadly diseases that were common in 1914. Sometimes Rachel wasn't feeling well. And sometimes Mrs. Carson didn't want her daughter to walk the half mile through snowdrifts to school.

Mrs. Carson had once been a teacher. Together they worked for hours on lessons so Rachel would not fall behind in her schoolwork. She especially loved her mother's talks about science and nature.

Their small house had only four rooms, so when her schoolwork was over, Rachel was glad to go outdoors. She roamed the 65-acre farm where she'd lived ever since she was born, on May 27, 1907. The Carsons owned a few pigs, horses, and cows, but Rachel's only farm chore was feeding the chickens.

There were no other children living close to the farm. Her brother and sister were so much older that

they were more like an aunt and an uncle than play-mates. Rachel could watch as her 17-year-old sister Marion practiced graceful dance steps in the parlor. Rachel wondered if she would ever be as tall or as lovely as her sister, or as smart as her brother Robert.

He would let Rachel watch as he tinkered with a new radio kit. At 15, Robert wasn't interested in play-ing games with her. Although Rachel was mostly alone and sometimes was lonely, she wasn't bored. Years later, she said of those who love science: "We are never bored. We can't be. There is always something new."

Rachel wandered along streams that trickled through the farm and beyond, to the deep woods. These creeks tumbled to the clear Allegheny River nearby. Only twelve miles downstream was grimy Pittsburgh, a city full of steel mills and coal smoke.

Following the woodland creeks, Rachel never knew what creatures she would find. She could watch a garter snake shed its skin. What would happen when the old skin rolled up past its eyes? She would wait patiently for her answers. Squatting close to the snake, she held her breath and watched as clear scales peeled off the snake's eyes and turned inside out with the rest of its old skin.

When Rachel had questions about animals, she would ask her mother. If Mrs. Carson couldn't solve the mystery for Rachel, she would show her how to find answers in science books. Rachel's mother looked stern, with her dark hair pulled tightly back into a bun and glasses perched on her nose. But she taught Rachel with love and gentleness.

They often wandered together through the woods. Once they found baby robins whose nest had been destroyed. They took them home to nurse, feeding them by hand every few hours. Within weeks, the robins took over the screened porch. The rest of the Carsons had to stay out until the babies learned to fly.

Rachel's father didn't mind being shooed off the porch. He loved the farm and the land, too. There was coal beneath their property, but he would not let coal-mining companies dig the riches of their land. The land, he told her, was all the wealth they had.

The Carsons weren't poor, but there was never enough money for extras. Mr. Carson sold some of their apples and earned money by helping other people buy and sell land.

Rachel's brother, Robert, looked at their land in a different way. He hunted in the woods and fields. Rachel went along on his hunting trips a few times. Robert showed her how to move silently through the woods. She practiced placing her heels gently on the ground and rocking forward onto her toes with each step as she followed him.

They looked like brother and sister, sharing the

same deep-set brown eyes and straight brown hair. There were big differences, though: unlike her tall and sturdy brother, Rachel was slender and small for her age. And she hated the killing part of those hunting trips. These were the same rabbits that Rachel had watched in the fields, the same kind that her favorite author, Beatrix Potter, had written about in so many books. In her soft voice, Rachel talked to Robert about his sport, arguing against shooting wild animals.

Wasn't it true that nothing on the farm except the pigs and chickens were killed? That gave them all the meat they needed. Their mother didn't even own a flyswatter. When an insect or spider wandered into the Carson kitchen, it was carried outdoors and set free. Rachel asked if the quick joy Robert got from killing was really worth ending a precious life for ever and ever. Her words made sense to him. He gave up hunting.

Robert and Rachel gathered with the rest of the family after dinner by the living room fireplace. A big bowl of apples from the orchard was always sitting on the table. The house had no electricity, and radio or television hadn't been invented yet. Some evenings they sang together while Mrs. Carson played the piano. Other nights, they listened as she read aloud.

With her mother's voice spinning stories and the snow whispering against the windows, Rachel would sink deeply into her chair. She would watch the light from the kerosene lanterns shimmer on the conch shell, and dream of the sea.

2

Big Plans

Rachel's life was the woods, her studies, and her dreams of the sea. In 1917, if a girl liked science, she was expected to be a nurse or a schoolteacher. Rachel did not want to be either.

Although it seemed to have nothing to do with nature, Rachel wanted to be a writer. "I have no idea why," she tried to explain later. "There were no writers in my family. I read a great deal . . . and I suppose I must have realized someone wrote the books, and thought it would be fun to make up stories, too."

Rachel, now a fourth-grade writer-to-be, read every

book in her house. When her father wheeled the buggy out of the barn and hitched up the horses, she would plead to go along to town so she could visit the library.

Each month, a magazine called *St. Nicholas* came in the mail for her. It was full of interesting stories, poems, and articles. Rachel liked the "*St. Nicholas* League" pages best. This section was written entirely by children and teenagers. Every one of those thousands of young writers became members of "The League." Only the best were printed.

Rachel wanted to see her own writing in *St. Nicholas*, but what would she write about? An idea came from Robert. The First World War had started in Europe, and the United States was getting ready to send its soldiers to join the battle. Like many young men, Robert joined the U.S. Army. In one of his letters, he reported a true story about a Canadian pilot who kept his plane flying after one of its wings had been shot off.

Rachel tried different words and sentences to see which best told this exciting story. She crossed out extra words. She read the story aloud to herself and made even more changes. Finally it was good enough to show to her mother. Mrs. Carson said it was ready to send to *St. Nicholas*.

After that, as each issue arrived, Rachel turned to the "*St. Nicholas* League" section first. Month after

month passed with no word about her article and no sign of it in the magazine.

By now the country was at war with Germany, and American men were fighting—and dying—overseas. Battle news filled the papers and came into the house over Robert's radio. Marion married and left the farm, but Rachel's life went on as usual. She read, walked the woods, studied—and waited.

Almost a year later, in the September 1918 issue, there it was: "A Battle in the Clouds, by Rachel L. Carson, Age Ten, Silver Badge Winner." She read again the pilot's story in her carefully chosen words:

He crawled out along the wing, inch by inch, until he reached the end. He then hung from the end of the wing, his weight making the plane balance properly. The Germans saw him and could not but respect and admire the daring and courage of the aviator, and did not fire until the plane had landed safely.

There was something else in the mail that month: a check from *St. Nicholas* for $10. The award was a lot of money in those days. Now Rachel knew she could be a real writer.

Her next submission to *St. Nicholas*, "A Message from the Front," was another battle story. Later she explained that, for her, good writing had always meant "hard work . . . writing and rewriting endlessly until you are satisfied that you have said what you want to say as clearly and simply as possible."

That kind of hard work paid off. Her second article won a Gold Badge from *St. Nicholas* in February 1919. A third piece, "A Famous Sea Fight," was printed that August, listing her as an "Honor Member" of the League.

Rachel had still another success with *St. Nicholas* while she was eleven. For her English class, she had written about why she liked *St. Nicholas* magazine. The advertising department of the magazine bought the essay and paid her a penny a word for it, which came to just over three dollars. This time the money was not a prize, but a *payment*. For years afterward, Rachel liked to say that she "became a professional at the age of eleven."

Rachel worked hard at school for the next few years, knowing she would need good grades to get into college so she could become a writer. Those years were full of changes for the world and for the Carsons as well.

After a long struggle, American women were finally allowed to vote. The very first radio station was on the air, and the U.S. Navy had sent an airplane all the way across the Atlantic ocean. The Carsons had a car now, and a bathroom indoors. Robert was away, working in Pittsburgh. And Rachel had to change schools.

Springdale High School stopped at the end of tenth grade. For eleventh and twelfth grades, Rachel went to Parnassus High School. It was a lonely place for her. Her mother had taught her to choose friends very carefully. Even when she was sure she liked a person, Rachel was too shy to make friends right away.

Rachel's new teachers were happy to have her in their classes. But Rachel's classmates were not so impressed. Rachel got to know some of them by playing field hockey. She liked being outdoors, and found that she liked the game, too. Rachel finally made the team in twelfth grade.

Schoolwork was still the most important thing in her life, though. Her classmates wrote a poem about her and put it beside her picture in the high school yearbook:

Rachel's like the mid-day sun
Always very bright
Never stops her studying
'Til she gets it right.

Now it was time for Rachel to choose a college. Mrs. Carson wanted her youngest child to study at an all-girl school near home. Pennsylvania College for Women, in Pittsburgh, suited Mrs. Carson. Rachel agreed. But they would have to find over a thousand dollars just to pay for the first year—money Mr. Carson couldn't spare.

The dean in charge of Pennsylvania College for Women wanted Rachel as a student. The school gave Rachel a scholarship, a gift of money. They helped her get a loan, too.

While Rachel waited for college to begin, she spent time in the woodlands around her home, hiking and camping. "I am never happier," she said at the time, "than when I am before a glowing campfire with the open sky above my head." She was filled with wonder when wild animals would creep close to her as she sat, patient and still, dreaming about her future as a writer. Rachel's life, however, did not turn out quite, the way she planned.

3

Writer or Scientist?

Rachel entered Pennsylvania College for Women in 1925, during the middle of the "roaring twenties." At last the war was over. Hems were raised to the knee for the first time. Businesses were growing. The whole country was in a playful mood—a mood 18-year-old Rachel could not share.

It was hard on Rachel, not having the money that the other girls did. It meant she couldn't have lovely new clothes. Even so, she always dressed with care. She wore only a touch of lipstick and her soft brown hair was held neatly with a barrette. She was slender and attractive. But when classmates invited her along to movies or to go out for sodas that she couldn't afford, Rachel had to make excuses. She felt lucky to be in college at all. And she told herself she was there to learn, not to play.

Rachel did everything she could to learn more about writing. She wrote for the student magazine and newspaper. As a reporter she had to talk to many important people. Rachel found she wasn't shy when she was working.

Rachel's English class teacher, Grace Croff, quickly became her favorite. Rachel was one of Miss Croff's favorites, too. It wasn't often that a student came along who showed such a gift for writing and also had the determination to become a writer.

Though Rachel had already decided to major in English, she had to take many other courses to earn her college degree. For her music course, she picked violin. She learned to play it well enough to get a B-minus. Rachel was one of the top ten students of her class by the end of the first year.

In her second year, Rachel had to take a science course. She didn't want to. Though she had always found nature exciting, her high school science classes had been dull. But Rachel found nothing dull about Miss Mary Skinker's biology class.

Miss Skinker led many field trips to state parks.

Once she took them to a spot where a hillside had been blasted away to make a flat space for railroad tracks. With hammers and chisels, the girls split apart layers of rocks. One dull gray piece broke open in Rachel's hands. Hidden inside was a fossil fish that once swam in an ancient sea.

To Rachel's surprise, she found the indoor science work with Miss Skinker exciting, too. Cutting open grasshoppers, starfish, and frogs showed Rachel the beautiful plan inside animals.

Now and then Rachel took a break from classes and schoolwork, when it didn't cost extra money. She played on field hockey, baseball, and basketball teams. One snowy night, she joined a sledding party on the hill by the dorm where she lived. Afterwards, she sang along with her classmates by the dorm fireplace.

For a party, Rachel bought a pair of silver dancing slippers. Always worried about her looks, Rachel chose shoes that were too small. They made her feet look nice and tiny, but they hurt. To stretch them, she had to wear the slippers around the dorm for two days so they weren't too painful for dancing.

The breaks were fun, but first on Rachel's mind were her studies. Her grades in Miss Croff's English class were excellent. So were those in Miss Skinker's biology class. In those days, people thought "the arts" were the opposite of "the sciences." They thought no one could be good in both. Rachel felt she had to choose between two fields, between two wonderful teachers, and between two careers. "I thought I had to be one or the other; it never occurred to me, or apparently to anyone else, that I could combine the two careers."

If Rachel switched to biology, there would be no more of Miss Croff's wonderful English classes. No more free time to write. Yet the beauty of science, the world of Mary Skinker, called to her.

One stormy night, Rachel sat alone in her dorm room, worrying over her decision. Hoping to calm herself, she reached for a book of poems. Sometimes Rachel wrote poetry and she had always enjoyed reading it. As the wind howled outside the windows, Rachel turned to Alfred Tennyson's poem "Locksley Hall." The storm and Tennyson's magnificent words wove their spell around Rachel. The hero in the poem doesn't know what to do, either. He thinks about running away forever to an island.

In the middle of the poem, Rachel stopped, caught by a beautiful line. "For the mighty wind arises, roaring seaward, and I go." Exhausted by worry and strain, Rachel read the line over and over. Thunder shook the old dormitory building. The wild beauty of the words, ". . . roaring seaward, and I go," echoed in her mind.

Thirty years later, she said, "I can still remember as that line spoke to something within me, seeming to tell me that my own path led to the sea . . . and that my own destiny was somehow linked with the sea."

Rachel had made up her mind. In the middle of that stormy night, she decided to turn her back on writing forever.

4

Against the Odds

Rachel's classmates thought she had made a stupid decision. "I've gotten bawled out and called all sorts of blankety-blank names," she complained to a friend. "Nobody can seem to understand why I'd give up English for biology."

There was no place for a woman scientist in the 1920s. The girls told Rachel she was throwing away sure fame as a writer to end up teaching biology in a small high school somewhere. It was no use. When Rachel chose a goal, nothing would change her mind.

Somehow she still found time to work on the school

newspaper. Now she was a copy editor, not a reporter. Her job was to fix mistakes other students had made in their spelling, writing, and word choices. It was careful, picky work and Rachel loved it.

Being a perfectionist, she was never happy until everything about her work was just right. Her school-work was nearly perfect, too. When she graduated she was at the very top of her class. Rachel's grades earned her two exciting offers. She said yes to both of them.

First she would spend the summer at a famous ocean-research center in Woods Hole, Massachusetts. She would work with real scientists at the edge of the sea. Then, in the fall, she would study at Johns Hopkins University in Baltimore, Maryland. They were offering her a full scholarship. Few women went to college in those days, and even fewer had a chance to earn a master's degree. But first, a summer at the seashore!

The ocean was even more wonderful than Rachel had dreamed. She loved the soft sea fogs that rolled over Woods Hole from the water. The beauty and power of what she saw sometimes moved her to tears.

One night she watched a school of young mullet fish rushing through a narrow tide channel. "I stood knee-deep in that racing water," she later remembered, "and at the time could barely see those darting, silver bits of life for my tears."

Rachel studied nature indoors, too. She had decided to find out about the nerves that go from a reptile's brain to different parts of its body. She gathered nerves from lizard and snake heads. Then she sliced, stained, and glued the nerves to hundreds of microscope slides. Hour by hour, Rachel was learning the patient ways of a research scientist. The summer was over before she could finish the project.

On the way to school at Johns Hopkins, Rachel stopped at the United States Bureau of Fisheries in Washington. She wanted to know just what she should study to get a job as a biologist.

Elmer Higgins told her about jobs with the government. He also let her know that the Bureau had never hired a woman scientist. But he wished her well and told her to come back and see him when she had her master's degree.

Rachel's chemistry and biology classes at Johns Hopkins started right after breakfast and went on till dinnertime. After that she had to study and work on the nerve project. And she had to do her own cooking and cleaning, too.

In the middle of the year, Rachel gave up her nerve project. She just couldn't get enough reptiles. She felt the discouragement all scientists feel when they have to give up after hundreds of hours of work.

Fish eggs were easier to get. Rachel decided to do a study of fish kidneys to earn her degree. Before fish hatch from their eggs, an early kidney grows. It works for a while, then disappears as the real kidney grows. Rachel made microscope slides of hundreds of codfish eggs to learn how the early kidneys changed.

Then, in 1929, the Great Depression began. The stock market crashed and many people lost all their money. Banks closed. Factories and stores shut down and millions of Americans were out of work. People were desperate, and families did anything they could to help each other out.

Rachel was lucky to have part-time jobs at two colleges, washing glassware and putting out the things students would need for their experiments. She rented a small house and invited her mother and father to live with her. It was cheaper than keeping both the farm and Rachel's apartment. Mrs. Carson did all the housework. Mr. Carson did "odd jobs" in town. Once he helped Rachel dig worms for a science experiment she was setting up for younger students.

Within a year, Robert moved in with them, too. His job in Pittsburgh had ended, and so had his marriage. He did part-time jobs to help the Carsons buy food. One place where he worked had no money left at all. They paid Robert with a cat. Rachel and Mrs. Carson were delighted. Cuddly, playful Mitzi made them laugh even in the grimmest times of the Depression.

At last, in 1932, Rachel finished her fish egg project

and a 108-page report to go with it. She had earned her master's degree. Now she could work as a scientist.

During the Depression, no one got the job of their dreams. Instead, they were happy to have any job at all. The streets were filled with long lines of people waiting for a chance to work or for a handout of free food.

In 1935, Rachel's father died. The Carson household was plunged into sorrow, and into desperation. Mr. Carson's odd jobs had helped them survive. Robert had moved away and Rachel was now the only support for her mother. She remembered Elmer Higgins's invitation and went to see him.

In Mr. Higgins's office, scientists were writing radio shows about fish. Most of them couldn't write without using fancy scientific words that were hard for others to understand. Elmer Higgins already knew Rachel was a scientist. He had one question for her: "Can you write?"

She got the job for $19.25 a week.

Rachel wrote the radio scripts well, but she needed a full-time job. To get a government job, Rachel had to pass a special test. She was the only woman who took the civil service exam for the job of fisheries biologist. Rachel scored higher than any of the men on the test. She was hired. After all those years, she was going to be a real biologist.

Elmer Higgins asked to have Rachel in his office. When Rachel showed up for work, he welcomed her warmly and described her new job. She would work in the Bureau of Fisheries—not as a biologist, but as a writer.

5

Roast Mice for Twelve

Rachel's office at the Bureau had only one window. She complained that it was "like working at the bottom of a well." Rachel did not like being indoors. But she did like the people with whom she worked on booklets and articles.

When they ate together in the office, laughter spilled into the halls. Rachel had a good sense of humor, but she showed it only to close friends like these. In public, she was cool and dignified.

She used her humor at the office to keep herself and others writing at their best. She asked her closest friend at the Bureau, Shirley Briggs, to draw cartoons of some of the bad writing they found. One writer had called a man who liked frozen fish "the man who was frozen-fish-minded." That made a strange picture! So did the "Raw Headless Dealers," a very poor way of describing men who sold raw shrimp with the heads taken off. Rachel hung the silly drawings up so others wouldn't make the same mistakes.

Once they found a government booklet of recipes for cooking wild animals. It was not only badly written, it was full of recipes no one would ever want to use. Even worse, it was mostly copied from someone else's book. They decided to play a trick.

They made up a telegram that said an important chef would like to visit the writer and try one of the recipes from her book. It told her to be ready one day the next week with enough roast mice to feed twelve people. They never did send the telegram, but it kept them laughing for months.

Rachel was serious about her own work. Soon after she joined the Bureau, Elmer Higgins asked her to write an introduction for a booklet about fish. She took such care writing it that she couldn't finish it that day at the office. Rachel wrote late into the night.

Her introduction, "Undersea," showed how animals live in the sea. Those living near coasts are ruled by rising and falling tides. Others, in the open sea, are swept about by endless currents. Still others live in the deepest ocean, never seeing sunlight. Rachel showed how all of these lives are forever connected.

Rachel was on time, as always, to work the next morning. How she wanted her boss to like "Under-sea"!

Mr. Higgins read it slowly, shook his head, and told her he wouldn't use it. Rachel was stunned. What was wrong with it? Her boss said it was just too good. It should be printed in an important magazine, like *Atlantic Monthly*, not in a little government booklet.

Rachel didn't have time for magazine work that year. Her sister, Marion, caught pneumonia and died. Rachel and her mother cried together as they tried to decide what to do about Marion's two little girls, Marjie and Ginny. Their father had died years earlier. Now the girls had no home. By 1936, money wasn't so tight, but would there be enough for four of them to live on? Mrs. Carson insisted that they had to try.

Rachel invited the girls to a larger house she had found near her job in Silver Spring, Maryland. She and her mother kept the house filled with laughter. There were visits to the woods and marshes of Maryland with Marjie and Ginny, to watch the birds and animals. But there just wasn't enough money.

Rachel began to sell articles about nature to the local newspaper. When everyone went to bed at night,

Rachel wrote more articles in pencil on the back of old office papers. After her mother typed them, Rachel sent them to many magazines. For months nothing sold, but she kept trying. Then *Reader's Digest* bought one about bats. Rachel made other sales. Finally she pulled out "Undersea."

It might have been "too good" for Mr. Higgins, but Rachel thought it still needed work. She rewrote "Undersea" again and sent it to *Atlantic Monthly*. They bought it. Rachel waited until the article came out in the magazine and handed it to Mr. Higgins as a surprise.

Again, she was the one who got the surprise. Her boss read it, and shook his head. What was the matter this time? Mr. Higgins said it ought to be a book, not just a magazine article.

He wasn't the only one who thought so. Quincy Howe, an editor at the Simon & Schuster publishing company, and Willem van Loon, a famous naturalist, both wrote to her. After she talked to them, Rachel went home to work on the book.

First Rachel made an outline, showing what she would write in every chapter. When she showed it to Mr. Howe, he gave her $250 and promised that he would publish her book. Every night the light in her bedroom stayed lit until she couldn't write another word. Two new kittens, Buzzie and Kito, kept her

company while the rest of the family slept. Sometimes she worked so late that even the cats fell asleep.

Rachel's book, *Under the Sea Wind*, told about the sea by telling the stories of the animals who live there—birds, fish, eels, and many others. It showed how their lives are tied together and to the vast ocean around them. Rachel made up some of the stories from facts she knew. Others were based on things she'd seen, like the rush of herring through the tide channel at Woods Hole.

After three years, the book was done. Quincy Howe was very happy with it. He told her that *Under the Sea Wind* would sell many, many copies. For each book that sold Rachel would get a royalty, a little bit of money. Those royalties would pay for all the years of work.

Another war had started across the Atlantic Ocean. It seemed certain that the United States would have to enter the war sooner or later. Men were once again joining the army, just as they had when Rachel was a little girl. Now she was 34.

When *Under the Sea Wind* came out, in November 1941, the newspapers told their readers it was an excellent book. No one cared.

On December 7, less than a month after Rachel's book got to the stores, Japan attacked the United

States, bombing American ships at Pearl Harbor, Hawaii. Americans were at war and everyone's life was changed.

6

The Sea Around Us

Under the Sea Wind sold very few copies. Rachel was discouraged. "Don't ever write a book," she told a friend at the time. "It doesn't pay as well as a single well-placed magazine article." Getting so little money for her work was upsetting, but having so few people read it was worse. Nothing was wrong with her book. There was just no time to read.

The Second World War kept the Fish and Wildlife Service (the new name for the Bureau of Fisheries) very busy. Battles were being fought by warships and submarines. These ships needed to know more about the ocean depths and currents. At work, Rachel read some of the fascinating reports from government research.

Other scientific news was horrible. Atom bombs had been dropped on the towns of Hiroshima and Nagasaki in Japan. It ended the war. It also ended the belief that life on Earth would go on, no matter what people did. Rachel had always thought "that the stream of life would flow on through time in whatever course God had appointed for it . . . without interference from one of the drops of the stream—man." Then, after atomic science proved her deepest beliefs wrong, Rachel said, "I shut my mind—refused . . . what I couldn't help seeing."

By 1947, Rachel was restless. Perhaps it was time to write another book, after all. She decided that this one would be "a book for anyone who has looked out upon the ocean with wonder," not just for scientists, but for "anyone who has stood on the shore alone with the waves and his thoughts, or has felt from afar the fascination of the sea." And it would have a gentle warning about how people must use their new powers carefully.

Soon after she started, Rachel found an agent, Marie Rodell. Marie's job was to help with all the business details of getting Rachel's new book into print. Marie found a publisher for Rachel's book. But Oxford

University Press said they wanted it in just ten months.

Rachel was not strong, and she was often sick. "Almost every year she had some fairly serious illness," Shirley Briggs remembered, "but she kept on going as best she could." Now that her mother was in her late 70s, Rachel was doing all the cooking and cleaning. After working long hours at the office and then at home, Rachel simply didn't have the time or energy to write a book quickly.

Rachel used parts of her job to help with her writing. She took an underwater diving trip with the Fish and Wildlife Service. The view through the windows of her diving helmet filled her with wonder. The sea was full of animals, riding with or fighting against or hiding from the strong currents. The ocean was as powerful as she had dreamed it would be, but so much more alive! She told a friend that the dive was one of the greatest moments of her life, "after which everything seems a little different."

Rachel became the first woman to see the northern Atlantic on a Fish and Wildlife Service research boat. Sailing for ten days without seeing land gave her a feel for the vast size and endless movement of the ocean.

These new adventures went into *The Sea Around Us*. Rachel used the exciting new facts learned from

wartime research. Every night she took so many books out of the library that she couldn't carry them all. An artist from her office, Bob Hines, helped. He was like a big brother to her, carrying books to and from her old green car. Experts the world over answered her questions through the mails. She used more than a thousand sources to find out what she needed to know.

After three years, Rachel was exhausted by the effort. "I am grimly determined to finish somehow." She complained to Marie when the book was nearly done, "I feel now that I'd die if this went on much longer." Finally it was ready. Rachel's mother typed it, and Marie sent *The Sea Around Us* to Oxford University Press in July of 1950.

Rachel's book began with "the gray beginnings of that great mother of life, the sea." Then she described the "long snowfall" of tiny bits of dead plants and animals who die in the sea. They sink down into deep, cold currents that sweep them back up to feed new life at the surface. Next, Rachel showed how tides, waves, and currents mixed the seas. Last, she explained how the oceans affect all of us. The message of Rachel's book was that the Earth, with its seas, is a balanced planet where nothing is ever wasted.

This is how we have learned to think of our world today. But in 1951, few people had ever heard the word *ecology*. Rachel wrote so clearly and so beautifully that others later thought the ideas and the writing were like poetry. Rachel answered that "if there is poetry in my book" it was only "because no one could write truthfully about the sea and leave out the poetry."

The publisher told Rachel that this new book would be a big seller and make a lot of money. That hadn't happened with *Under the Sea Wind*, and she didn't believe it would happen this time, either.

Before *The Sea Around Us* was printed, Marie sold parts of it to *The New Yorker*, an important magazine. One of the chapters won a $1,000 prize. And *Reader's Digest* offered her $10,000 to sell her book through its book club.

The Sea Around Us arrived in bookstores in July. By August, it was on the best-seller list. By Christmas, there were 4,000 copies *a day* being sold. Many people were so touched by the writer's knowledge and love of the sea that they wanted to meet her and to hear her talk. That part was hard on Rachel.

One evening at a college where she was to give a speech, she looked so unhappy that a friend asked her if she was all right. "The truth is," Rachel answered, "I'm much more at home barefoot in the sand or on shipboard in sneakers than . . . in high heels."

Even so, Rachel found herself giving speeches to thousands of people. And, though she had always kept her life private, newspapers sent reporters to find out more about her.

This was fame and Rachel did not like it one bit.

7

Fourteen Dead Robins

Now that Rachel was famous, Marie decided to get *Under the Sea Wind* printed again. This time it became a top seller, too. Having two books on the best-seller list ended Rachel's money worries forever.

She paid all her debts and quit her job. She had a house built beside the sea in West Southport, Maine. In the summers, she could write there in peace and quiet. Her front yard was full of wildflowers and sweet-smelling balsam fir trees. A few steps from her back door were a granite cliff and tide pools full of sea animals. Rachel could see both the woods and the water from the desk in her workroom. There she began work on a new book.

It wasn't easy. Her best-selling books got many awards. Rachel had to give many speeches, though she was still nervous about talking to groups. She wrote out exactly what she was going to say each time so she wouldn't make any mistakes. Then she changed words and sentences to make her speeches sound even better. When the writing was just right, Rachel underlined or put stars beside the parts that were most important. That way, she remembered when to make her soft voice a bit louder.

Whenever she could, Rachel traveled along the Atlantic seacoast, taking notes for the new book, *The Edge of the Sea*. Once she bragged that she and her mother had driven 2,000 miles in just a few months. Muffy, a favorite cat, traveled with them. They visited coral beaches in Florida, sandy beaches in North Carolina, and her own rocky Maine coast. Rachel wanted to know which animals lived where, and why.

The Edge of the Sea needed many drawings. Rachel asked Bob Hines, the Fish and Wildlife artist, to illustrate her book. Rachel had a close friendship with Bob, but not a romance. She said she never had the time for dating or for marriage. Her friend Shirley added that, with an elderly mother and two nieces to support, "Rachel had a lot more family responsibilities than many married people."

Bob joined Rachel, her mother, and Muffy in their wanderings up and down the Atlantic coast whenever he could. He drew pictures of the live animals Rachel found. Often when she was working, Rachel forgot all about time. She would stand for hours in icy-cold tide pools in Maine, watching tiny animals. Sometimes her legs would get so numb she couldn't walk. Bob would pick her up like a stack of books, and carry her back to the warmth of her car.

Then Rachel would head back to Silver Spring or to Maine to write and rewrite the book. She described hundreds of the animals she had seen on coral, sandy, and rocky beaches. She explained how the animals' lives were shaped by these different environments. And her book showed the readers that they, too, fit into an environment.

In October of 1955, *The Edge of the Sea* reached bookstores. It was another instant best-seller. Everyone wanted to meet the famous Rachel Carson. Her fans found her in beauty parlors when her hair was up in curlers. They even knocked on her hotel room door before she was dressed in the morning.

Only in tiny West Southport, Maine, could she relax. Rachel had become close friends with her neighbors, Stanley and Dorothy Freeman. Rachel and Dorothy shared a love of nature, fine music, and the sea. Rachel's niece Marjie often came on visits to Maine with her son, Roger. She was ill with arthritis and needed help with her little boy. When Roger was a baby, his father had died. Now Rachel was like a loving grandmother to him. Some of Roger's first words were the names of seashells that Rachel had shown him as they walked along beaches.

From their times together, she wrote a magazine article about sharing nature with children. The most important thing for them to learn, she wrote, is "a sense of the beautiful, the excitement of the new and the unknown."

Then, early in 1957, sickness swept the family. Marjie and Mrs. Carson had pneumonia and Rachel caught the flu. Rachel and her mother fought off their illnesses, but Marjie died. Suddenly, 50-year-old Rachel had a lively 5-year-old boy to care for, in addition to her own 89-year-old mother. It was harder than ever to find time to write.

When the Freemans' grandchildren came to play with Roger, Rachel would lead them all down the steps behind her house to the ocean. "Rachel answered all their questions. A microscope always sat ready in the living room for closer looks at the animals they found," the children's mother remembered. "Before we could have snacks, we had to carry everything back down the steps to the water and put each animal right back where we had found it."

There were fireworks shot from Rachel's rocky cliffs on the Fourth of July, and many nature walks through the quiet Maine woods. But Rachel the writer was restless. The strain of family problems, fame, and her own poor health were wearing her out. She needed a new project to give her life a fresh direction.

The idea came in a letter. A friend wrote to tell her of the horrible deaths of fourteen robins after a bug poison, DDT, was sprayed over her yard. Could Rachel do something?

In the 1950s, chemical companies were allowed to sell almost any kind of poison to kill bugs, weeds, molds, and other pests. Millions of tons of these pesticides were used.

Many scientists were worried. What were all those poisons doing to other animals, to the soils, and to the seas?

Rachel decided to write an article. No magazine would print it. They didn't think her facts were right. The chemical companies had told everyone that their poisons were safe. So had the government. Yet the more research Rachel did, the more upset she became.

The poisons were spreading through the world, making people and animals sick. If people knew how dangerous the poisons were, they wouldn't buy them anymore. They would be angry with the people who made them and with the government that said pesticides were safe. The powerful companies that made pesticides would fight to keep her story quiet. The Department of Agriculture would argue that she was wrong.

But somebody had to warn the world. Somebody who was both a scientist and a writer.

Was sharing the truth worth the battle Rachel knew she would face? "Even knowing that it would force her into the spotlight, a role that she hated, she was sure she was right," a friend remembered. Rachel *had* to write the book.

8

The Final Battle

Rachel kept her new book, *Silent Spring*, a secret. The book had to be as strong as it could be before its enemies found out about it. Rachel double-checked every fact. She asked other scientists to read parts of the book to be sure she was right. And she asked them to help her keep the secret of *Silent Spring*.

The pesticide problem was worse than anyone knew. In the 1950s, most people had never heard of pollution. They believed that the government would protect them from any danger. Rachel was learning that this was not true.

Scientists had made dreadful poisons that could end all life on Earth. If people kept using these chemicals, springtime might someday come silently, with no birds left to sing, and no people left to hear them. The more Rachel learned, the more determined she was to write the book. It wasn't easy for her.

A neighbor remembered that "Rachel would do all the household chores first and try to take care of the family, and then she would try to find time to work." Twice a year, everything was moved to Maine or back to Maryland. It was no wonder that work on *Silent Spring* went slowly.

Rachel stopped writing in 1959. Her mother, very old and very ill, died. Mrs. Carson had helped shape nearly all of her daughter's life. She had taught Rachel to love nature and encouraged her to be a writer. She had helped with every decision Rachel had ever made. Except for a few years when Rachel was at college and during the war years, they had always lived together. Now, for the first time, Rachel was alone. It was a terrible shock.

A few weeks later, Oxford University Press told Rachel they wanted to publish *The Sea Around Us* again. They asked if she would add some of the new facts that scientists had learned in the ten years since her book had first been published.

Rachel went back to writing, working through one

illness after another. First it was the flu, then a painful stomach ulcer. Arthritis and infections in her knees kept her from walking for months. An eye infection made her blind for a few weeks. So many bad things were happening that Rachel said she felt like she was under an evil spell that would never let her finish *Silent Spring*.

Worst of all, she learned that she had cancer, and that it was going to kill her. Another person might have given up writing, but Rachel said, "Knowing the facts as I did, I could not rest . . ."

Now she studied about cancer, as well as pesticides. These facts went into new chapters about how poisons in the environment cause cancer. Did she have time to finish *Silent Spring*? She had to. All life on Earth was in danger, not just her own.

Early in 1962, *Silent Spring* was done. After four years, the article no one would publish had grown into an enormous book, beautifully written and full of complicated scientific ideas. But would it work as a warning? Would it make people want to change things? Marie sent *Silent Spring* to Rachel's publisher and to *The New Yorker* magazine. Rachel wanted to hear what the editors thought.

Within a week, she got a late-night phone call. Mr. William Shawn, editor of *The New Yorker*, had just finished reading her work. He couldn't wait until the next morning to tell her how wonderful it was. He was horrified by the things he had learned from *Silent Spring*. How could this have happened? What could be done about it?

That was exactly what Rachel wanted to hear. She knew now that *Silent Spring* would work. Rachel picked up her cat and walked stiffly into her study. In spite of all her sickness, Rachel had reached her goal. Finally she could rest. She put on a classical record, sank into a deep chair, and cried with relief.

Rachel didn't get much of a rest. When parts of *Silent Spring* were printed in *The New Yorker* a few months later, it shocked the whole country. Readers sent thousands of angry letters to newspapers, to the chemical companies, and to the government. As Rachel had expected, pesticide makers were furious.

Men from the chemical companies and the Department of Agriculture argued with her in newspapers, magazines, the TV, and radio. Some tried to prove her facts wrong. Others said she didn't know enough about science to understand the things she was writing about. One said, "Her book is even more poisonous than the pesticides."

President John F. Kennedy asked for a special report from top scientists to decide who was right. When the report came out, it agreed with Rachel. New laws were made to limit chemical pollution in the United

States and to find other ways to control insect pests.

Awards and offers to travel and speak flooded in to Rachel. She was too sick to do very much. She worked to make her article about children and nature into a book. She never finished it, but *The Sense of Wonder* was published after she died.

Even though she was in pain most of the time, Rachel agreed to be on television. Many thousands of people had read her book, but on TV, she could tell millions more about the danger of using too many pesticides. On the same show, a man from a chemical company tried to prove she was wrong. Rachel was still a nervous speaker, but she knew her facts were true. She said, "Man is a part of nature, and his war against nature is . . . a war against himself." The viewers believed her.

Silent Spring was published in dozens of other countries in 1963. No matter what language it was printed in, the message was the same: We must be more careful about what we do to the Earth. Around the world, new laws were made about pesticides.

Rachel spent the next summer in Maine. One afternoon, she and Dorothy Freeman sat at the top of a rocky cliff near Rachel's house. They listened to the sounds of the sea below them and watched monarch butterflies heading south for the winter. As the but-

terflies danced along the cliff's edge, Rachel and Dorothy wondered how many would ever be back. Most would never live to return, they realized. The two friends were not sad about it. That was how life was for butterflies.

Later that day, Rachel wrote a note to explain to Dorothy what "those fluttering bits of life taught me this morning." She said she had found a "deep happiness" in knowing that "it is a natural and not unhappy thing that a life comes to its end."

A few months after Rachel returned to Silver Spring, her own life came to its end. She died on April 14, 1964. But the work of her books went on.

Her writings about the sea showed how all life was tied together. *Silent Spring* showed how the future of all life depended on what we do. Over the years, Rachel Carson's love of nature and her beautiful writing have helped to change the way a world of people looks at the life of their planet.

About This Book

Rachel Carson has always been special to me. Reading her books as a teenager helped me decide to become a scientist. After years of teaching, I am now a writer. Working on this book has made me feel closer to the woman who meant so much to me.

I talked to Rachel's friends and read books about her. At a library at Yale University in New Haven, Connecticut, I held the pages she wrote and rewrote. I listened to tapes of her speeches and read through boxes of her careful research notes and letters. In Maine, I stood in the pine-scented room where she wrote *Silent Spring* and I found starfish in her tide pools. And I read, again, her powerful books.

Our world is safer because of the pollution laws passed after *Silent Spring* was published. But there are still many people who do not believe that what we do to nature, we do to ourselves. Pesticides are still being misused. Rachel's life may be over, but the fight to keep our Earth safe is not.

K.V.K.